Delegating Work

20 MINUTE MANAGER SERIES

Get up to speed fast on essential business skills. Whether you're looking for a crash course or a brief refresher, you'll find just what you need in HBR's 20-Minute Manager series—foundational reading for ambitious professionals and aspiring executives. Each book is a concise, practical primer, so you'll have time to brush up on a variety of key management topics.

Advice you can quickly read and apply, from the most trusted source in business.

Titles include:

Creating Business Plans

Delegating Work

Finance Basics

Getting Work Done

Giving Effective Feedback

Innovative Teams

Managing Projects

Managing Time

Managing Up

Performance Reviews

Presentations

Running Meetings

2🕐 MINUTE MANAGER SERIES

Delegating Work

Match skills with tasks
Develop your people
Overcome barriers

HARVARD BUSINESS REVIEW PRESS

Boston, Massachusetts

HBR Press Quantity Sales Discounts

Harvard Business Review Press titles are available at significant quantity discounts when purchased in bulk for client gifts, sales promotions, and premiums. Special editions, including books with corporate logos, customized covers, and letters from the company or CEO printed in the front matter, as well as excerpts of existing books, can also be created in large quantities for special needs.

For details and discount information for both print and ebook formats, contact booksales@harvardbusiness.org, tel. 800-988-0886, or www.hbr.org/bulksales.

Copyright 2014 Harvard Business School Publishing Corporation

All rights reserved
Printed in the United States of America
10 9 8 7 6

The web addresses referenced in this book were live and correct at the time of the book's publication but may be subject to change.

Library of Congress Cataloging-in-Publication Data

Delegating work.
    pages cm. — (20-minute manager series)
  Includes index.
  ISBN 978-1-62527-223-2 (alk. paper)
1. Delegation of authority.   2. Workflow—Management.
3. Management.
  HD50.D447 2014
  658.3'128—dc23

                                    2014000381

Preview

Whether you're newly promoted or a veteran leader, you've got a team to direct, goals to meet, ideas to pursue, an abundance of enthusiasm—but not enough time. Overloaded with tasks that "only you" can handle, you never seem to get to the long-term planning, staff coaching, or other higher-level management work that you'd like to do.

You can't add more hours to your day, but improving your delegation skills can help you make the most of the hours you have. Becoming more effective at delegating offers advantages for you, your team, and your organization by improving productivity, reducing stress, enhancing staff skills, and increasing morale and motivation.

This book provides an introduction on how to:

- Create an environment that fosters successful delegation.

- Overcome your concerns about delegating.

- Know what (and what *not*) to delegate.

- Match assignments to skills and interests.

- Provide the appropriate level of support and oversight.

- Transfer your knowledge of successful delegating to others.

Contents

Contents

Delegating Work

Why Delegate?

Why Delegate?

D o you find your growing responsibilities and workload outstripping your available time? Are you spending much of your day completing tasks below your level of skill and authority— such as providing project updates or compiling data on new clients—work that could be performed by others on your team? Do you lack the bandwidth for higher-level pursuits, such as analyzing your department's short- and long-term resource requirements, implementing a training program for new hires, or developing process improvements to speed order turnaround time?

Delegating—assigning tasks, projects, or functions to another person—can reduce the demands on your time and allow you to develop your leadership skills while improving organizational productivity and giving your employees opportunities to extend their capabilities. Delegating well is managing well; not relinquishing authority, but *leading*.

As you review the purpose and benefits of delegating, remember that it's not just about the payoff for you—it's about the benefits for your staff and your organization as well.

The purpose of delegating

When you delegate, you transfer the responsibility for performing a task, completing a project, or executing a function to another person. You still retain authority, control, and responsibility with regard to the larger work, but the person to whom you delegate—

a direct report, team member, outside contractor, or maybe even a peer—tends to the details.

For example, you might task a senior project manager with compiling a weekly update of all projects in your unit and confirming that your internal standards, client specifications, and regulatory requirements for each project are being met. This individual obtains project status information, but you still manage the direct relationships with clients and other unit heads who are working with you on the projects.

Delegating can have a profoundly positive effect on employees and the organization as well as on the manager who delegates, yet overworked managers often underutilize this tool.

The benefits of delegating

Delegating work offers an upside for everyone. Let's take a closer look.

Benefits to you

In addition to reducing your workload and stress level, delegating improves your coaching skills and likely boosts your job satisfaction. Cleaving off tasks that others can accomplish, such as running expense reports or drafting the employee newsletter, will give you more time to focus on work that requires your particular skills and authority, such as working with the finance director on your group's revised quarterly forecast, assembling a team to assess the impact of a rival's recent expansion into new markets, or developing a communications plan for your company's reorganization (and the necessary but difficult staff changes that will accompany it).

Benefits to your direct reports

By delegating to people on your team, you increase their motivation and confidence and help them develop new skills. Say you need to cut a few days out of your production schedule. Rather than documenting the current manufacturing process yourself, you ask a member of your staff to take on this task. Your employee gets the opportunity to have a voice in the change process while also learning how to plan work, enlist the cooperation of others, assume responsibility, and gain experience with managerial activities. Some delegated tasks also offer direct reports greater exposure within your organization or industry—such as when you tap a member of your staff to speak at a conference or to organize a panel of experts for a networking event.

Benefits to your organization

Assigning work to the right people at the right level maximizes an organization's resources, improving productivity and saving the company money. Your organization benefits from both the improved skill levels of your staff members and your ability to get more high-level work done. Effective delegating also develops trust—you rely on your staff person to get the job done, and they look to you for support and guidance as needed—and trust within organizations means more-engaged workers. Finally, delegation strengthens communication, as you and your staff member find new ways to work together and as your staff person learns how to influence others to complete the assignment.

Delegating is also an effective way of assessing staff members' capabilities before offering promotions. Suppose, for example, that you'd like to see if Carlos, a junior member of your engineering team, is ready for a project manager position that is opening up. Assigning him to lead a small project, such as overseeing the redesign and production of a component with a high failure rate, will help you judge his suitability and help him assess his comfort level in that capacity in a fairly low-risk way. If you and Carlos agree that additional training is advisable before he can be promoted, you can work it into his career development plan.

. . .

To achieve these benefits you must not only delegate but do so *effectively*. This book shows you how.

Building a Foundation for Effective Delegating

Building a Foundation for Effective Delegating

A re you spending more time "doing" and less time managing?

If you always seem to have too much rudimentary work to do, or if you find yourself on the job nights and weekends trying to keep up with endless lower-level administrative tasks, assigning some of your work to staff members could help you free up some time for other higher-level activities, such as prepping for an important board meeting or policy development.

If you *are* delegating but you're regularly interrupted by direct reports who have questions about their assignments, or if you often need to intervene in delegated tasks or projects because of missed deadlines or budget overruns or overrule staff decisions and personally redo poorly executed assignments, you could benefit from honing your delegation skills. Perhaps you've been directed to offload some of your work to a colleague you now must oversee—a scenario that requires well-tuned delegation skills and finesse. Finally, if your employees complain when you delegate work, if morale in your group seems low, or if turnover is high, it might be time to move from just delegating to delegating *well*.

In this book we'll walk you through the fundamentals of choosing the right work to delegate, preparing to delegate thoughtfully, making the assignment crystal clear, and monitoring progress effectively. But throughout that process you'll also want to address big-picture needs, such as creating an environment that fosters productive delegation, establishing management practices that promote delegation, and banishing your own concerns and fears about delegating.

Establish the right environment

Creating a workplace that encourages and supports delegating can help you gain cooperation from your staff. Here are some tips to help set up the right atmosphere, especially as you make and communicate the assignment.

Making the assignment

When you delegate work, you're more likely to rally enthusiasm and support from your staff if you consider the following as you balance assignments:

- Delegate entire projects or functions when possible—not just portions—to help increase your employees' motivation and commitment.

- Avoid assigning only tedious or difficult jobs. While it's sometimes necessary to share grunt work, like database entry, on larger projects, try to balance the less desirable jobs with tasks that captivate staff and might gain recognition for your employees, such as representing the team at a trade show.

• Give your direct reports the resources needed to get the job done. And think in broad terms: Resources could be people (additional staff or simply an introduction to someone they'll need to work with), tools (such as software or training), information, or development opportunities—anything that can help employees learn, resolve issues, and handle assignments on their own.

• Delegate to people whose judgment and competence you trust. Your ability to select the right person reflects your decision-making and goal-setting skills.

• Develop trust in less skilled staff members by delegating highly structured assignments to them (such as compiling production and delivery figures for your quarterly report).

- Provide possible career advancement for staff members by delegating work that involves face time with your manager or with a high-level manager in another division.

Communicating the assignment

Open lines of communication set the foundation for an effective delegation culture. Try to incorporate the following tips into your delegating practice:

- Make certain that your staff knows *what* is expected of them and *why* the task is important to the unit and the organization. People are more motivated when they understand the reasons for doing things a certain way and when they recognize the importance of their work. Linking projects to larger initiatives also helps build a sense of shared responsibility for the unit's overall goals. For instance, you might explain to your employees that immediately updating the client database with revised order status information (rather than making daily or even weekly updates) helps ensure that all members of the team have access to the latest figures and can respond accurately to client queries—thereby meeting your organization's targets for customer satisfaction ratings.

- Articulate goals, expected outcomes, and measures of success. Also, create clear guidelines for follow-up, monitoring, and feedback. Having detailed conversations about these issues up front minimizes wasted time and resources and ensures that the work will be completed successfully—and allows you to hold your staff accountable.

- Cultivate independent thinking by asking questions rather than dictating orders. Encourage your people to come to you with problems, but groom them to also bring their own ideas, observations, and possible solutions. Open-ended questions—"What things might we consider if we implement the solution you're proposing?"—help motivate employees to think (and to reveal the degree to which they have thought about problems and assignments on their own). When they raise a problem with you, ask them what they've already tried to do to solve it (or what they've considered doing), along with the pros and cons of their proposed approaches.

- Urge your staff to share their interests as well as their availability for new projects.

- Acknowledge that mistakes can be made, that delegating is a learning experience for you and your staff. Offer instruction or coaching as needed.

Building a workforce open to delegation will also help make you a better delegator. Fostering the right culture for delegation with existing staff is important, but you can also contribute to that culture when hiring additional staff members. Look for applicants who not only are qualified for the specific job but also are willing to grow, take on new tasks, learn from their assignments, strengthen their skills, and make informed decisions. Selecting people who are more than just their job descriptions will allow your unit to make its best contribution to the organization overall. Be creative in your pursuit of ideal candidates. For example, ask vendors and customers who know your staff and your organization to recommend potential new hires.

Giving yourself time and space to think also has an impact on the delegating culture you're creating. Continually answer the question, "What next?" Your unit can't deliver top performance without a clear picture of where it's going, so once you've envisioned your unit's future, share it with your team so everyone is clear on—and energized by—your major goals and how you'll achieve them. Take time to reflect on what's happening in your company and industry, explore new ideas, and get excited about the possibilities of the future. Block off thinking time on your calendar during periods when you're at your best—perhaps first thing in the morning or a specific afternoon each week—and be sure to record, sort, and save your thoughts. Or take advantage of a long commute to write down your ideas (if you're on public transportation) or record them (if you're driving). This reflection time isn't for preparing for meetings, drafting reports, or handling other day-to-day matters. It's open time to *think* and be creative.

Building a workplace culture that embraces delegation is an important step, but you may still have uncertainties about your role. The next section takes a look at some common misgivings about delegation.

Address your concerns

Despite the benefits to all involved, many managers still feel uneasy about delegating. For instance, you might fear that by assigning your work to others you'll abdicate responsibility and lose control because you've relinquished day-to-day oversight. Or, pressed for time, you might elect to do a job yourself rather than teach someone else how to do it. If this is your first leadership role, you may be reluctant to delegate the types of tasks that gave you your star power, such as mentoring junior employees. If you've been a leader for a while, you might shy away from delegating because you've had a bad experience with it, such as a staff member not taking responsibility for assignments or missed deadlines. Gaining proficiency at delegating work can take time and experimentation, but over the long run your fears should dissipate as you hone your skills and your staff gains confidence and expands its capabilities.

The proper mind-set can help you overcome these common concerns:

- *It's just easier to do it yourself.* The thought of organizing, explaining, and monitoring an assignment can feel like it will add hours to the job that you just don't have. But that's a short-sighted view. The comparatively brief amount of time you spend planning to delegate will likely be worth it, since over time your employees will be able to take on more responsibility for structuring and planning their own assignments. Say you groom a couple of junior employees to track regulatory changes that affect your industry. As their sense of ownership grows, your time will be freed up for other initiatives, such as winning (or attracting) new clients.

- *You're having a difficult time transitioning from specialist to generalist.* You loved your functional job. You excelled at it. That's why you were promoted. So when you think of delegating some of your work, you're reluctant to give up the very tasks for which you've become known—and likely enjoy doing. However, you're not saying goodbye to your knowledge and experience—those will be critical as you guide your staff members through their assignments. Take a new product introduction as an example: You might not be developing and executing the marketing plan, but you'll be leading your team as they brainstorm and start the launch process, guiding them around obstacles, and giving them the benefit of your experience.

- *But everyone knows you're the expert.* If your direct report surpasses your skill set and becomes the go-to person in your specialty area, what will happen to your reputation? Maybe you've taken great pride in developing your expertise in projecting the return on investment for new client services. Everyone knows you're the first person they should talk to when they have a great idea they're convinced will boost the bottom line. You may hesitate to pass that baton, especially while you're still developing competency in your new role. It's normal to feel competitive or uncertain while you're transitioning long-held and deeply valued knowledge, but developing your people will serve your organization by widening the pool of available experts (in this case, experts on evaluating client service revenues) and help you grow into your role as their leader. Plus, when your direct reports look good, *you* look good.

- *You lack confidence in your staff.* Start by delegating small tasks and projects so you can gradually build their confidence—and your own. For example, you might ask a staff member to make arrangements for a client visit—

reserve and set up the conference room, order lunch, and organize a tour of the facility—and afterward publicly show your appreciation.

- *You can't identify a staff member with the skills needed for a particular assignment.* Train or coach an employee to develop the skills required, "borrow" a staff member from another group, hire a temporary worker, or explore dividing the assignment into tasks (or subtasks) that one or more of your employees could handle. For example, perhaps you need a financial analyst for end-of-the-year reports for your unit, and the finance department has some IT work your staff can perform: Make a trade.

- *You like things done your way.* Focus your energy on communicating your preferences and quality standards rather than on controlling how the tasks will actually be completed. For example, maybe you organize project files strictly by date, but your employee prefers to arrange them by topic. Your employee's approach may get the job done *and* demonstrate a different way to tackle the work.

- *You believe your staff will resent additional work.* Don't just dump grunt work on your people—manage their expectations with open discussions. Let them know they'll get opportunities to do new and interesting work. Tell them how projects will expand their capabilities and that you'll support them in making their own decisions—and then follow through. When you do have to assign dull administrative work or a beastly project, such as organizing a cluttered image library, be up-front about it: Acknowledge that it's beneath your employee's abilities but that it has to be done. Give the reasons why: Providing the larger context will lessen the sense of drudgery and motivate your employee to complete the work without resentment.

- *You know you could quickly complete a task an employee is struggling with.* When you see someone spinning his wheels trying to extract information from the company knowledge base, it can be hard not to jump in and take over. But trust your staff member's ability to get the job done. Practice keeping silent. Give him a chance to muddle through and figure it out. Be available to provide support, but allow your employee a chance to learn. Interceding could cause frustration for you both—and cost you the time you'd hoped to save.

With your concerns about delegating now in check, you're ready to prepare to delegate a project.

Preparing to Delegate

Preparing to Delegate

You may have a general idea about the project or task you'd like to delegate, but before making an assignment you'll want to do some prep work. You'll need to note your reasons for delegating, determine exactly what work to hand off (and what *not* to), decide how large a slice of the work you'll delegate (just a task or an entire function?), and specify the skills required to successfully complete it. Next you'll identify the best person for the assignment and determine the level of authority to be delegated. Following all these steps may seem like overkill, but doing so will ensure that you make the right assignment to the right person for the right reasons—and with a high probability of success. Let's walk through each step.

Consider your reasons for delegating

As you're mulling over work you could assign to someone else on your team, take a moment to review *why* you're looking to delegate. What do you hope to achieve? Do you simply want to decrease your workload, or do you need to off-load lower-level administrative jobs so you can concentrate on a specific project, such as assessing the effectiveness of your staff's interactions with clients? Perhaps your objective is to motivate your team members and improve morale by increasing their levels of responsibility or helping them extend their capabilities into new technologies and processes. Maybe you have a combination of reasons.

Carefully thinking through why you're looking to delegate will help you set clear goals when you make the assignment and more easily assess how well you've achieved your purpose once the assignment is complete. Goals in mind, you're ready to start flagging specific pieces of work you could delegate to others.

Determine what (and what *not*) to delegate

As you assess your workload to see which tasks, projects, or functions you might delegate, consider:

- *Jobs that others could readily do.* Although you probably enjoy some of the tasks that fall into this category, which can make them hard to give up, be open to delegating them. For instance, assigning a small task from an important project to a new employee eager for advancement—such as logging bugs and fixes as a project moves through development— could motivate her while providing you with insight on how well she follows through on assignments.

- *Jobs that require specific training or experience.* Delegating this type of work can give staff members interesting and challenging opportunities. For example, training a reliable team member to take over your role on an interdepartment task force would increase the employee's collaborative and technical skills, as well as his visibility.

For jobs you deem too important to delegate wholesale, consider ways you might share the responsibility with someone. Could you subdivide a task, project, or function so you handle a discrete part and delegate the rest? The following examples illustrate the importance of flexibility in determining what to delegate:

- Marisol, a department head, decided to share responsibility for a software evaluation project that has companywide impact.

She asked Larry, a member of her team, to request proposals from potential vendors and to track what came from where. Marisol then enlisted Larry's help in reviewing the proposals by asking for his feedback, but she took the ultimate responsibility for evaluating the proposals—and for making the final choice of vendors.

- For a number of years, Yuan designed, administered, and documented an annual employee job satisfaction survey. After his promotion to manager, however, he lacked the bandwidth this sizable project demanded. Siphoning his time and energy from more pressing responsibilities and sacrificing his weekends to work on the project didn't seem like attractive options. Yuan's solution? He formed a task force. Under his leadership and oversight, Emma and Kervin, two direct reports with solid analytical skills, took on the most time-consuming parts of the job, such as survey development and coding. When the final survey report was circulated within the company, Yuan shared the credit for its successful completion with Emma and Kervin.

For jobs seen as boring or unpleasant—cleaning out files and making cold calls come to mind—promote collaboration and a supportive environment by dividing tasks among your staff members *and* doing a few yourself. Also, use the delegation of less desirable work as a chance to seek input from your staff about the types of assignments they *would* find appealing.

Not all work, however, can or should be delegated. As a manager, you must retain responsibility for activities such as the following:

- Directing and motivating your team

- Aligning your team's strategy with company goals

- Evaluating employee performance

- Helping your direct reports develop their careers

- Hiring and firing staff members

- Handling complex customer negotiations

- Performing tasks that require your specific set of technical skills

Once you've identified the type of work you'd like to delegate, you need to consider how much of it you'll turn over. Will you delegate just a single task (asking someone to pull a list from the customer database for an e-mail campaign)? Or an entire function (conceiving and implementing the marketing plan for your company's new service)? Let's review your options.

Choose how much of the work to delegate

You have a general sense of the kinds of things you want to hand off, but as you narrow your options down, consider how much of the work you'll transfer:

- *Delegating by task.* Assigning specific tasks or subtasks, such as writing a report, conducting research, or planning a meeting, is the most basic approach. You'll probably want to start here.

- *Delegating by project.* Assigning a group of tasks designed to achieve a specific objective is a broader approach than task-level delegation. Delegating by project—for example, developing a new employee handbook, conducting a customer survey, or training employees on a new computer system—increases the scope of the assignment and generally requires a staff member who can handle a wide range of responsibilities.

- *Delegating by function.* Assigning groups of tasks and projects related to one ongoing activity, such as sales, marketing, or training, involves delegating a particular function to one staff member who will provide you with regular updates within that function. For example, you might assign your resident IT expert oversight of networking systems for all projects.

Now that you have a good idea of your goals and you've identified both the type and extent of work you'll be delegating, you're ready to assess the skills that are needed to ensure the project's success.

Identify the skills required

Before selecting the person for a given assignment, analyze the job and determine the skills it requires. During your analysis, answer these questions:

- What kinds of *thinking skills* are needed for this job? Does the work require problem-solving ability, logical thinking, decision making, planning, or creative design?

- What are the *activities* that must be performed for the assignment, and what *systems* or *equipment* will be needed? Do the activities include creating a new database, for instance, or organizing, training, or developing?

- What *interpersonal skills*—such as negotiating with suppliers, conducting interviews with experts, or handling delivery complaints with customers—are needed to complete the assignment?

To illustrate this kind of analysis, assume your group has been asked to customize the user manual for the company's new intranet so employees in various departments—from R&D to production to sales—will know how to use the features most relevant to their jobs. It's a corporate-level project with company-wide visibility, but the deadline is way too imminent for you to undertake the project alone. Shauna, a bright, energetic new hire with manual-writing experience, has offered to lead the effort. It seems like a perfect opportunity. But before assigning it to her, you carefully evaluate what's involved and identify exactly what skills the project demands. Through this process, you realize that the project requires deeper skills than Shauna has at this point, although they are skills she has explicitly told you she wants to develop. So instead of delegating the entire project to her, you establish a project team with a more senior lead than Shauna and try to match her skills with specific project tasks that support the larger project. Her work on those tasks will then inform future assignments and help you identify training opportunities for her.

When you have a number of assignments to delegate, it can be helpful to make up a log or spreadsheet on which you can specify your criteria for each proposed item: expected results, deadline, milestones, skills required, and so on. Use this tool to match people to jobs and to uncover where training might be necessary. This activity will also help you track how often you're using any one person for various types of jobs so you can better balance the dream assignments—and the drudgery.

Select the most suitable person

Once you know what's required for a task, project, or function, review the strengths and weaknesses of your staff. Recognize that not all skills are transferable to all situations (for instance, a great telephone sales representative may freeze in a face-to-face situation).

As you compare the skills required with the characteristics and capabilities of your staff members, keep these factors in mind about each person being considered:

- *Growth and development.* In what ways could the work address the expressed interests and

needs of your staff members to try on new roles
or take on stretch assignments?

- *Development of new skills.* Consider how an
  assignment might challenge a staff member to
  expand his competencies.

- *Availability.* You may want to avoid choosing
  an employee whose work on a more critical
  project would be interrupted.

- *Previous assignments.* Try to delegate tasks
  even-handedly among your staff members to
  help improve the skills of each, as well as to
  avoid the appearance of favoritism.

- *Assistance required.* Determine how much
  help would be needed from you for successful
  completion of the assignment and how much
  time you have available.

- *Time on the job.* Don't give new employees
  extra assignments until they're fully settled in.

Avoid delegating only to those people you know will accept added work without complaint. Reliable staff members may be flattered by your confidence in them, but without proper compensation or recognition, continually delegating to the same individual—even a willing one—can lead to resentment, absenteeism, and even defection.

As you contemplate your options, don't hesitate to take advantage of the skills of more than one person. When you have a pool of resources to choose from, pairing people with complementary skills can help you achieve the best results:

- Ask a staff member with great people skills to conduct telephone interviews with customers and a staff member with great analytical skills to examine the feedback and compile data.

- Have a person with excellent writing skills draft the text for a new brochure and a person with graphics and production skills complete the layout and manage the final printing.

Routinely keeping track of the special skills of your staff members—and logging their skills into the spreadsheet discussed earlier—will help you match people to assignments. For example, someone who can simplify abstract concepts might be a good person to conduct database implementation training, whereas an employee with good organizational abilities might be a suitable choice for overseeing warehousing operations. Also, to make the best use of staff resources and build your employees' capabilities, delegate to the lowest possible skill level required.

When considering whom to assign work to, don't overlook people beyond your own group—and don't forget your supervisor or your peers in other groups as possible resources. In some instances you may save time and money and gain needed expertise by assigning work to talent *outside* your organization, such as freelancers, consultants, or other temporary workers.

Here's an example of how your selection process could play out: You'd like to ask Anil, an experienced, logical-thinking member of your staff, to research how customers are using a high-profit-margin electrical component your company manufactures. His objective would be to learn about possible new telecommunications applications. In addition to being familiar with the industry, Anil has mastered the people skills necessary to mine the data and to communicate his findings to engineering and marketing managers. The more you consider Anil, the better you feel about him as a candidate, yet you know there are other variables you should take into account. Anil's availability is one: He's expressed the desire to take on this time-consuming project, but his existing workload is heavy. In addition, you'd need to provide him with extra help from within your team to ensure the project's successful completion. If you believe Anil is interested but too busy, but you still feel he's the right person for the job, you might reassign some of his current project work to another team member, or you could give Anil primary responsibility for the project and suggest that he get help from one or two other staff members (say, to sort and compile the data he obtains).

Now that you have the right person, you'll need to determine what level of authority to grant him to allow effective execution of the assignment.

Decide on the level of authority to grant

The level of authority you choose to grant should depend on the requirements of the assignment, the employee's capabilities, and your level of confidence in the person you've selected. To determine the kind of authority you'll grant to your employee:

- Assess the employee's past performance in making decisions.

- Consider the consequences of wrong decisions, and decide what degree of risk you're willing to take.

- Determine the minimum amount of authority your employee will need to complete the assignment successfully and efficiently. (You wouldn't want the employee to have to come to you for approvals every step of the way.)

Several options exist along the broad spectrum of authority. You can decide that your employee may:

- Make and implement decisions as needed without prior consultation with you.

- Make decisions as needed, but notify you before implementing them.

- Make recommendations for a final decision, which you must then approve.

- Provide you with several alternatives, from which you'll make a final decision.

- Provide you with relevant information, from which you'll develop alternatives and then consult with your employee to reach a decision.

What might granting a specific level of authority look like in real life? Say you place Cy in charge of approving purchase orders for your unit. You specify a dollar limit within which he has free rein and a range of expenses that he can approve but must report to you. For all other purchase orders, he must research alternative products or services and review the requests with you.

In addition to granting a specific level of authority, you can eliminate confusion and encourage initiative and problem solving by delegating *responsibility* to one person rather than dividing it among a number of people—even if you are delegating the *work* to a number of people. Make sure every person involved clearly understands who is ultimately responsible for the outcome. For example, you might assign the responsibility for reviewing, approving, and submitting expense reports to one of your employees, who, in turn, asks a colleague to follow up with finance to ensure that reimbursements are made on time. Regardless of how follow-up is delegated, your direct report remains responsible.

Now that you've determined what to delegate to whom, and at what level of authority, you can proceed to the next step: actually assigning the work.

Making the
Assignment

Making the Assignment

For your delegation to be successful, you must thoroughly describe the job and your expectations to the person who will be taking on the work. Take this employee's point of view as you communicate the scope and authority of the assignment to make sure you're transferring all the necessary information. Equally important to the success of your delegated work is how well you communicate the scope and authority of the assignment to the other members of your team.

Discuss the work with your staff member

Spend some time going over the details of the job, ideally in a face-to-face meeting. To gain trust and avoid misunderstandings, discuss all aspects of the assignment. Clarify your specific expectations, and get the employee's commitment to the project.

In this important meeting, you'll:

- *Describe the task, project, or function.* Clearly state the purpose of the work. Explain how it fits into the big picture for your team, your unit, and your organization. This may be obvious to you, from your place in the hierarchy, but it may not be obvious to your employee.

- *Introduce background material.* Review any reading, spreadsheets, data, or other materials or content that the employee will need to complete the work.

- *Identify the resources and support available.*
  Determine what support the employee will
  require from you. If special training or coaching is needed, discuss how it will take place.
  Explore the need for additional materials
  and/or staff to meet the goals of the assignment.

- *Establish a feasible timeline with agreed-upon
  deadlines.* Get your employee's buy-in to make
  sure the timeline is achievable. Consult the
  schedules and availability of other key play-
  ers and factor in your employee's existing
  responsibilities.

- *Explain the level of authority you're granting.*
  Use examples to establish clear guidelines for
  when the employee can act independently and
  when consultation with you is required.

- *Agree upon standards of performance, measures
  of success, and levels of accountability.* Set
  firm metrics for quality, time, cost, and other

variables. Underscore the employee's account-ability in meeting these standards.

- *Determine a process for follow-up and feedback.* Establish a protocol for regular progress reports, including their frequency (weekly or monthly) and method (e-mail, staff meeting, or one-on-one with you). Set up parameters for your ongoing feedback.

- *Discuss your possible involvement.* Specify how and when you will become involved if the expected goals of the task, project, or function are at risk or if other major problems arise.

Outlining the details of the work to be done and how and when you'll communicate about the assignment will set your delegation up for success. Talking with your staff member ahead of time about how you'll monitor the project and deliver any feedback will make your role seem less intrusive once the work is under way.

Follow up your meeting with a memo outlining the key points of the discussion. Better yet, ask your employee to prepare a summary memo. This will give you an idea of how well your employee understands the assignment.

Communicate with your team

Take the lead in communicating to your team the scope of the delegated assignment, plus any other relevant information. Your clear and transparent message will deflect resentment and competitiveness on the part of other staff members. Your forthright attitude and openness to discussion will help build their trust in you.

Consider this example: To support your projections for long-term office space requirements, you've assigned Michael, a friendly and outgoing junior employee on your team, the task of collecting information on the work preferences of each person in your group. If you fail to communicate Michael's role in this project *before* Michael begins asking everyone personal questions—such as whether they like to work on-site or off-site, whether they work more productively with scheduled hours or with flextime, and if they feel the need for scheduled staff meetings—you could inadvertently cause unfounded rumors and disruption within your team.

With the assignment made and communicated to the team, it's time to monitor the work. You'll need to give support and feedback without micromanaging— a fine line you'll learn to walk in the next chapter.

Monitoring the Assignment

Monitoring the Assignment

O nce you've delegated the work, shift into monitoring mode to ensure that everything goes as planned; don't just assume all is going well until you've heard otherwise. You'll want to check on how the work is progressing, provide support if needed, and anticipate and address any problems without hovering or hounding.

Track the delegated assignment

Regularly check progress to make sure the assignment is on track to be completed correctly and on time. Confirm that all interim milestones—which you discussed with the employee when you made the assignment—have been met. Saying something like "I'll need to see the proposed design revisions by next Friday" reflects your proper control of the work as manager; adding "Let's meet Wednesday to see how you're progressing and discuss any problems" signals that you're monitoring the work and prepared to offer guidance if necessary.

Depending on the number of tasks and the complexity of the delegated work you're overseeing, consider using one or more of the following tools to facilitate monitoring:

- A file folder for each assignment

- A tracking form or log (what, who, milestone dates, deadline, and so on)

- A large wall calendar or dry-erase board

- Verbal updates in staff meetings

- Written status reports, delivered on a pre-arranged schedule

- Project management and tracking software

- Online collaboration tools and shared calendars

Close monitoring gives you opportunities to provide coaching and feedback. Keep in mind, however, that the ultimate goal is successful and on-time completion—not *how* the work was done. Monitor the assignment without micromanaging, allowing your employee to learn and grow as he or she tackles the work. Above all, support your staff member both when things are going well and when mistakes are made.

Provide support

While monitoring an assignment, continue to provide support, but without being intrusive. These tips can help you strike the right balance of feedback and follow-up:

- Notify the appropriate individuals of the authority you have granted your staff member in delegating this assignment.

- Review resource needs, and ensure that appropriate supplies are available.

- Continue to provide any information that may have bearing on the assignment, such as reference materials, reports, or changes in plans or procedures.

- Point out any potential difficulties you may see, based on your experience with similar projects.

- Clarify when you want to be involved, such as when it looks as though a commitment won't be met or when major problems—such as a misunderstanding with a peer—arise.

- After the work begins, intercede with advice or directions only if requested.

- Remember to focus on results and not on the methods or approach used to achieve them.

The following example illustrates a productive technique for providing support. Jessica decides to delegate the upcoming launch of a line of business productivity apps for tablets to Jamil after determining that he has the required skills. Jamil knows business productivity software well and has worked on product launches for device apps before (although he hasn't led one). He also likes working independently and is eager to prove himself. As the weeks pass, Jessica sees steady progress and is pleased with Jamil's sensitivity to the strategic timing of the launch. She's pleased, too, that she has more time for her other projects. By chance, however, Jessica discovers that the marketing group, which is integral to the success of the product launch, is overtaxed with other work. She could mention her concerns directly to the marketing group, but she's worried that doing so might make Jamil feel as though she's taking back responsibility for the launch. How can she best support Jamil while ensuring that the launch is carried out successfully?

Because Jamil doesn't have as much experience as Jessica does in dealing with problems in a product launch and may not know how to handle the competing marketing deadlines, Jessica elects to point out to him the possible difficulties she sees based on her experience with similar projects. In that discussion—taking care not to undermine the authority delegated to him—she supplies him with the information she learned about the marketing group, "because it may have a bearing on the assignment."

The sensitive manner in which Jessica provided support to Jamil helped him address the situation independently without undermining his authority or consuming a lot of Jessica's time.

Anticipate and address problems

Be alert to early signs of trouble. If your employee hits a roadblock (for example, a manager from another department refuses to provide data) or begins to fall behind (maybe a strike slows parts delivery), it may be necessary to intervene. You don't want to solve every problem that employees encounter in their assignments—that would defeat the purpose of delegation—but do use coaching, encouragement, and added resources as you see fit to help them help themselves.

When an assignment falls off track, take the following steps to right it:

- Create a plan of action and a timetable for addressing the problems. Work with your staff member to make sure your solution is realistic, and have the employee agree to the plan once it's final.

- Offer additional resources (such as staff or funding), if available, to provide assistance.

- Complete *selected* parts of the assignment to lighten the load on the employee, set an example, and ensure success.

- Delegate upward (advocate to upper management on behalf of your staff member) when escalation is necessary for a successful outcome. For instance, you might need to ask your boss to deal with the manager mentioned earlier who would not share their data.

While addressing problems, be on the lookout for *reverse delegation*, which can occur when a staff member to whom you've delegated an assignment either wants to return the entire job to you or, more likely, subtly shifts it back onto your plate by expecting you to solve problems and make decisions. Resist the temptation to step in. Instead, continue to help your employee complete the job.

For a deeper understanding of how reverse delegation can hobble you, imagine this scenario: You're racing down the hall, late to a meeting. One of your less experienced project managers, Chrysanthi, stops you and says, "We've got a serious problem on that project you assigned me last week." She quickly outlines the issue. You don't have the information to make an on-the-spot decision, so you quickly reply, "Let me think about it." You've just allowed what *Harvard Business Review* authors William Oncken Jr. and Donald L. Wass famously called a *monkey* to leap from Chrysanthi's back to yours; you're now working for your subordinate. A better response would have been to ask Chrysanthi to draw up possible solutions, make a recommendation, and then brief you. Employees try to hand off monkeys when they lack the desire, ability, or confidence to confront them. Helping employees develop needed problem-solving skills can be more time-consuming than tackling problems yourself, but it saves time in the long run, and it fosters the development of a trusting relationship. When you encourage employees to handle their own monkeys, they acquire new skills—and you have time to do your own job.

The following strategies can help deflect reverse delegation and keep assignments moving:

- Encourage the employee to come up with her own solutions or options.

- Help the employee assess the situation.

- Confirm your confidence in the employee's ability to make decisions.

- Provide positive reinforcement for the work done so far.

- Provide coaching to help the employee refine new skills.

In some situations, such as a missed deadline, you'll need to reassess your staff member's ability to successfully complete an assignment. Support the employee, but provide assistance only as necessary. Avoid placing blame for difficulties beyond your employee's control, but make sure she takes responsibility for mistakes that are clearly her own. And remember that mistakes should be viewed as growth opportunities rather than punishable offenses. Only in extreme cases—say, when failure to meet established goals will have a serious negative impact on other projects— should you consider rescinding the delegation.

Each delegation you make can be a learning experience—for you and for others in your organization. Next we'll look at assessing completed assignments and sharing what you learn with others.

Review the Process

Review the Process

U se what you learn from each delegation to increase your effectiveness in assigning work to your staff and others, as well as in teaching delegating skills to your colleagues.

Evaluate completed assignments

As delegated assignments are completed, take the time to reflect on what worked and what didn't. Jot down what you would do differently next time.

Next, schedule a debriefing with the person you delegated to, and review lessons learned from this assignment. These guidelines will help you use what you discuss to improve future delegation:

- Ask for feedback on how the assignment worked out.

- Recognize achievements and provide positive reinforcement for tasks done well.

- Compare results with the agreed-upon deadlines and expectations.

- Avoid criticism and blame for any problems, but discuss possible improvements for future projects.

- If appropriate, create an action plan to support your direct report's growth through ongoing coaching or supplemental training.

Finally, take steps to ensure that the person you delegated to receives recognition—not only from you, but from others who benefited from the successful completion of the work, including your peers, your manager, and members of supporting teams.

Teach delegating skills to others

Developing your staff is as essential to your job as achieving your group's financial goals. When you don't take advantage of delegating opportunities, you block the advancement of your staff, which can leave them resentful and disengaged.

Consider how you might share delegating skills you've learned with other team leaders in your unit or division—in particular, newly designated managers. The following suggestions can help you strengthen delegation skills across your organization:

- *Lead by example.* Trust and empower rookie team leaders by delegating to them, which in turn should make it easier for them to delegate assignments to their direct reports.

- *Encourage risk taking.* Show, by example, how taking small risks to play to staff strengths pays off. Early successes build confidence.

- *Identify what to delegate.* Help team leaders divide complex projects into manageable chunks with clear milestones.

Becoming proficient at delegating work can enhance your effectiveness as a manager, open opportunities for your staff members, and benefit your organization. Seek out additional information on delegating, and continue to sharpen your skills.

Learn More

Articles

Birkinshaw, Julian, and Jordan Cohen. "Make Time for the Work That Matters." *Harvard Business Review*. September 2013 (product R1309K).

More hours in the day: It's one thing everyone wants, and yet it's impossible to attain. But what if you could free up significant time—maybe as much as 20% of your workday—to focus on the responsibilities that really matter? The authors have spent the past three years studying the productivity of knowledge workers and discovered that these individuals spend, on average, 41% of their time on activities that offer little personal satisfaction and could be handled competently by others. On the basis of their research, the authors have come up with a process to help knowledge workers make themselves more productive. It involves thinking consciously about how they spend their time, deciding which tasks matter most to them and their organizations, and dropping or creatively outsourcing the rest. The tasks to be dropped are sorted into quick kills (things you can stop doing now, without any negative effects), off-load opportunities (work that can be delegated with minimal effort), and long-term redesign (work that needs to be reconceived or restructured). Once the tasks are disposed of, the freed-up time is spent focusing on more important work. When 15 executives tried this method, they were able to reduce desk work by an average of six hours per week and meetings by two hours per week. They filled the time with value-added tasks such as coaching and strategizing.

Maruca, Regina Fazio. "Fighting the Urge to Fight Fires: A Conversation with Carl Holmes." *Harvard Business Review.* November–December 1999 (product F99605).

In this concise Forethought piece, Carl Holmes, formerly chief of the Oklahoma City Fire Department, discusses the difficulty in handing off responsibility when you've worked your way through the ranks. It's tempting to perform the very tasks you're supposed to be overseeing, but delegating responsibility is a critical part of being a good leader. Nowhere is that more evident than in firefighting, where efficient leadership can mean the difference between life and death. Holmes describes the radical steps he took to get his battalion chiefs to stop fighting fires and instead start doing their real jobs: managing their people. His insights offer valuable lessons for any new manager seeking to master delegation.

Oncken, William Jr., and Donald L. Wass. "Management Time: Who's Got the Monkey?" *Harvard Business Review.* November 1999 (product 99609).

In this classic article, the authors show what can happen when reverse delegation is allowed to run amok. Managers who can't resist stepping in to solve employees' problems or who take back a delegated task end up having no time to carry out their own responsibilities. Oncken and Wass (as well as Steven Covey, in an afterword to the article) offer numerous suggestions for cultivating a sense of initiative in your employees, so they develop the skills and confidence required to handle their own problems rather than transferring them back to you.

Walker, Carol A. "Saving Your Rookie Managers from Themselves." *Harvard Business Review.* April 2002 (product R0204H).

Most organizations promote employees into managerial positions based on their technical competence. But very often, that kind of competence does not translate into good managerial performance. Many rookie managers fail to grasp how their roles have changed: that their jobs are no longer about personal achievement but about enabling others to achieve; that sometimes driving the bus means taking a backseat; and that building a team is often more important than cutting a deal. Even the best employees have trouble adjusting to these new realities, and that trouble can be exacerbated by the normal insecurities that may make rookie managers hesitant to ask for help. Walker, a coach and management consultant, addresses the five problem areas that rookie managers typically face: delegating, getting support from senior staffers, projecting confidence, thinking strategically, and giving feedback. You may think these elements sound like Management 101, but these basics are also what trip up most managers in the early stages of their careers (and even, Walker admits, throughout their careers).

Books

Hill, Linda A. *Becoming a Manager: How New Managers Master the Art of Leadership*. Boston: Harvard Business School Press, 2003.

For many novice managers, learning to delegate and develop people, rather than carry out tasks themselves, is difficult. In this book, Hill examines the wide range of challenges people face when they move from an individual–contributor or entrepreneur role to a managerial role for the first time. Hill shares excerpts from interviews she conducted with new managers and provides her own insights, based on years of research. She puts a human face on managers learning to be managers, showing readers that they're not alone and helping them see that delegating can be mastered.

Hill, Linda A., and Kent Lineback. *Being the Boss: The 3 Imperatives for Becoming a Great Leader*. Boston: Harvard Business Review Press, 2011.

You never dreamed that being the boss would be so hard. You're caught in a web of conflicting expectations from subordinates, your supervisor, peers, and customers. You're constantly fighting fires. You're mired in office politics. You end each day exhausted and discouraged, wondering what, if anything, you've accomplished. You're not alone. As Linda Hill and Kent Lineback reveal in *Being the Boss*, becoming an effective manager is a painful, difficult journey. It involves trial and error, endless effort, and slowly acquired personal insight. Many managers never complete the journey. At best, they just learn to get by. At worst, they become terrible bosses. This book explains how to avoid that fate by mastering three imperatives: (1) Manage yourself: Learn that management isn't about getting things done yourself; it's about accomplishing things through others. (2) Manage a network: Understand how power and influence work in your organization, and build a network of mutually beneficial relationships to navigate your company's complex political environment, and (3) Manage a team: Forge a high-performing "we" out of all the "I's" who report to you. Packed with compelling stories and practical guidance, *Being the Boss* is an indispensable guide, not only for first-time managers but for all managers seeking to master the most daunting challenges of leadership.

Keenan, Kate. *Management Guide to Delegating*. London: Oval Books, 1999.

In this short and informative book, Keenan provides a comprehensive overview of the key elements of delegation. Topics include determining why and what to delegate, deciding who can do it, briefing and monitoring, and understanding attitudes about delegating. Each chapter concludes with a list of questions, as well as tips for improving delegation skills.

Luecke, Richard A., and Perry McIntosh. *The Busy Manager's Guide to Delegation.* New York: AMACOM, 2009.

Delegation amounts to a lot more than just passing work off to subordinates. When handled correctly, it gives managers a chance to strengthen their departments by developing the skills and organizational competencies of their people. Filled with quick tips, exercises, self-assessments, and practical worksheets, this book presents an easy-to-master five-step process for effective delegation. Readers will learn how to determine which tasks to delegate, identify the right person for the job, assign the tasks, monitor progress and provide feedback, and evaluate performance. The book shows readers how to set the stage for excellent results, what to do if things go wrong, and how to ensure that all their people benefit from the experience. This is a quick, comprehensive course on an essential—and sometimes overlooked—management competency.

Sources

Firnstahl, Timothy W. "Letting Go." *Harvard Business Review*, September–October 1986.

Harvard Business School Press. *Delegating Work: Expert Solutions to Everyday Challenges*. Boston: Harvard Business School Press, 2008.

Harvard ManageMentor. Boston: Harvard Business School Publishing, 2002.

Johnson, Lauren Keller. "Are You Delegating So It Sticks?" *Harvard Management Update*, July 2004.

Keenan, Kate. *The Management Guide to Delegating*. Horsham, UK: Ravette Publishing, 1996.

Maddux, Robert B. *Delegating for Results*. Menlo Park, CA: Crisp Publishers, 1990.

Oncken, William Jr., and Donald L. Wass. "Management Time: Who's Got the Monkey?" *Harvard Business Review*, November 1, 1999.

Walker, Carol A. "Saving Your Rookie Managers from Themselves." *Harvard Business Review*, April 2002.

Wilson, Susan. *Goal Setting*. New York: AMACOM, 1994.

Winston, Stephanie. *The Organized Executive: A Program for Productivity*. New York: Warner Books, 1994.

Index

Notes

Notes

Notes

Notes

Notes

Notes

Notes

Notes

Notes